E written

By Lou Rhinehart

ISBN 978-0-6151-3976-0

Nobody does it all by themselves.

That is another of the things I wish I'd been able to talk more about with my father. It is his love of language that I inherited.   My thanks go to my sister Susan and her husband Bob for their patient love and support. Jen and Lauren Merritt were great help in allowing me to invade their home and for leading me through the techno-jungle that is self publication. My mother was my best sounding board and critic, as well as my most ardent cheerleader. I thank you, Mother. There are others who's assistance has been invaluable. Unbeknownst to them, theirs have been the faces I've seen when writing or theirs the lyrics or tunes in my head. I thank them all the same.

Lou

E.

Enough emotional energy evolved to entice our Elvin friends elsewhere.

Everyone except Errol eliminated eel from their eating exercises.

Even the elliptical evince elaborately entertaining elements.

Erudite eunuchs elevate esoteric excreta to new levels of excellence.

English Environmentalists enhance evening-wear with electroplated encephalopods.

Eying eastern elephants excites erratic Engineers.

Ectoplasm for Everyone.

Evangelical enunciation elicits envy from uneducated audiences.

Elastic eight-balls engage in eccentric entertainment.

A small sampling of words beginning with E. English is rife with them. I should say American English is rife with them. Many terms of description begin with E. We have everything from Elegant to Easy to describe someone. Erratic, erstwhile, ethnocentric, energetic. They can apply to all of us. Think of it. How many E words can you come up with and how many of them can you hang on yourself?

We all have our Es. This work is intended to touch yours. It is a celebration of My language, of it's color and it's brilliance. A celebration of the human spirit and our wonderful ability to turn and twist and bend our language to fit whatever occasion. I speak so highly of American English only because it is the language with which I am most familiar. I know, in the right hands (mouth?), any language can be as beautiful and efficient as mine and I hope my ideas can survive the translation.

So, this work goes out to the Es in all of you. Just a touch, from me to you, to let you know there's someone else here.

-Lou
08/15/06

1

CLIFF DIVER

Imagine yourself perched atop a cliff,
high above the waters of the Pacific.
The waves crash against the rocks in a heaving mass of white
and the spray reaches you even here.
The rhythmic ebb and flow of the waves is hypnotic,
and the breeze, at this height, is cool and stiff.
 As you watch, the water flows out and out and out.
The Maelstrom below recedes and recedes, and you leap.
Your arms spread to embrace the sky,
toes pointed, back arched, you plummet,
 and the water recedes.
Far below, where the water line scores the cliff,
you see the rocks and canyons shrouded in moss.
The jagged spines run down to the sand,
so flat and so far away.
In the air, time is meaningless;
 and having leapt, the die is cast.
 ...and reality slips into slow motion.
 The waters flow out and out and the talus inches closer.
The wind screams past your ears and presses gently on your chest
and stomach.
 There's an eddy at your back and your hair dances there,
tickling and stinging your flesh.
And, in these eternal seconds,
you know the water will not return.
 And you fall,
with such speed it pulls the air from your lungs, and yet, there's no
sense of falling.
The light and color play off the rocks in greens and grays,
and diamonds of water fall sparkling in the sun.
Through wind-blown tears your eyes strain to see the beauty of the
approaching stone, and the waters move out and out.
Now, far below the water line, you see the mountain close.
Shells of white and pink race past amid blooms of red coral and green
leaf.
The gray stone glistens almost black and white diamonds dance
flashing by.
You're close now.
You can see the sand you'll never reach
and the ridges that stand up to catch you.
How long have you fallen?
 days, weeks, years?
or, has it only been seconds?
 And the waters flow out and out.

2

CANDLE

Years ago, I predicted the end of the world.
I put it far off, in the future,
past my lifetime.
I saw fire, and explosions,
mushroom-clouds and millions of people
dying by degrees.
I saw generations of damaged children,
and centuries of rebuilding.
And I saw the fall come again.
The old ways, our ways,
came again to the fore.
I saw it as cyclic, as recurring again and again,
until finally, the bombs were enough,
...the fires...
The poisoned Earth shook us off like sated parasites
I see now, I was wrong.
In my naivety I had expected a comparatively quick end to the
violence.
I had expected the loss of millions upon millions over the first year,
then, death by the hundreds of thousands for a few more.
From then on, a curtailing.
I saw the population grow strong again.
Conquer the elements, build homes, build cities.
I saw them build machines.
On other nights, in other dreams,
I saw man pulled from the rubble.
I saw his wounds dressed and his tears dried,
Then I watched him search through the wreckage
to rescue the living and bury the dead.
Beyond that vast graveyard, on the distant horizon,
shone the light of a single candle.
....I never really saw the taper, only it's glow,
so tiny and flickering, so far away.
But, you know how you know in dreams,
As well as I know my own name,
as well as I know I was me, even yesterday,
I know what shines in that candle's light.
...It is a child before whom lies an open book.

ARTISTS

What is it that sets the artist apart from society?

Is it his choice? Is it that he sees the world differently than those about him? Is it his demons?

What values or fears fence him off from the world?

The sculptor, the painter, the musician, the poet, we all have our isolation in common.

The world is not right for us, nor are we right for the world. Our peers are few and far between. We seek them when we are in need of solace, when we are in doubt of our own validity.

The day to day trials of life have no meaning for us. So too, do the laws and rules of our day lack value in our eyes.

It's not that we respond to a higher calling. We leave that to priests and politicians.

We answer to only the truth.

Our work is laid beside it and compared and its value is deemed in that light.

When our work strikes the basic chord common to all mankind, when a smile of understanding lights the eyes of the beholders, when their heartbeats fall in sync with the rhythm of the drum or the stroke of the brush, then does our work have merit.

It is not those who speak of our work that we strive to please. Rather, it is those who feel a chill run down their spine or goosebumps rise on the back of their arms that we hope to effect. It is the most basic of human emotions we hope to reach.

Seeing truth in the works of Dali and Picasso as well as in that of Michael Angelo is a thread we share.

When we are pressed to awed silence by the music of Wagner or the words of Poe, when the artist speaks only to us and we are the only ones to hear, when our hidden hopes and fears are spoken by another, it is then that we are in the presence of greatness.

It is to them that we compare ourselves, to their work that we compare ours.

Truth, like beauty, is timeless.

Venus de Milo has not paled over the centuries, nor have the words of Socrates lost their sting.

Moonlight Sonata evokes tears today as often as it ever has and Da Vinci's Last Supper still pulls the same heartstrings.

The thread that runs common through all these works is truth and in that truth lies beauty.

So, we go on walking our paths alone ignoring the whispers and stares of the rabble.

We work and work, and dig within ourselves for that perfection we've found in the masters. We strip ourselves of our armor and costume and lay our throats bare for your knives.

We hope, above hope that we will touch that string within you and make that silent chord resound.

DOORWAYS

This is not at all what I expected. In fact, I expected nothing. Nothing, at all.

The pain in my chest is gone. I can breathe.

There is light, but it's dim. I can see I'm in a hallway.

I can't see the end, just doors, one after another, after another, on both sides, as far as I can see.

There is a chill and the air feels damp, like after a heavy rain. Light shines across the hall from below every portal and I hear the sound of a million voices, all whispering.

My death, like my life, held no great surprise.

I knew full well, the end had come. My material wealth has been disposed and all loose ends have been securely tied.

There is no one my departure will grieve overmuch and there is nothing I've left behind that the world will remember. It was my intent to stop, to enjoy an eternal, senseless sleep. It was not this.

I still have my body, although it feels young and stronger than it has in years. I can see my hands before my face in the faint and shifting light.

My legs carry me and my ears are touched by the sounds.

There are scents in the air and they mix and blend and no one sure thing can be identified for long.

There is cinnamon and sulphur and the hint of rose, the warm scent of blood mixed with arctic wind that foretells of coming snow.

For so long I was convinced there would be nothing here, there would be no here.

I was wrong.

Now, how many of my other beliefs will I find mistaken?

What lies behind these doors? What is this place? I see no others along the darkling way, but surely I can't be alone.

In life, I had no thought of facing decisions, here. I had felt that by now, all decisions would have been made and no more choices would be offered. I thought that all the choices I'd made in life would lead to certain death. And that death would be the end of choice, that there was no more to decide. I had thought death would be the end and eternity would go on without me.

Now I find myself here? And what of these doors?

Am I to open them, am I to step through? And which door?

For the first time there is fear. Everything I knew was wrong.

Now I ask if my choices have all been in error. And what of the choices I make now? No door is marked.

Which will open on heaven and which on hell? Is there reincarnation behind one, is there purgatory?

Who's voices do I here? Are they of those in my life that died before me, or those who have died since time began?

Is it the choir of angles or the tormented souls of hell or, could they all be the same?

As I pass I hear each is different.

Through this one I hear the murmur of soft voices, but no word is distinct. From this one come the sounds of machinery, a distant bang and clunk of metal on metal.

The next is silent and the light that crosses it's threshold is cold and clear.

Still, I can see nothing. I dare not open any of these.

Not yet, not yet.

Across the hall the first door vibrates with the bass of some smoky rock tune that I just can't remember the name of, the light under the door is blue and flashes.

The next is silent or is it?

I press my ear and far beyond the wood I hear the cry of a child, and the distant barking of a dog.

I lurch for the child and grasp the knob in flight, then am stayed. What does it mean to open this door? If I go through will I be able to come back?

But the child, the child, it cries.

And what else lies beyond? Eternity? Am I choosing mine by breasting this gate?

But the child, it cries, it cries. The dog, it howls.

Enough! The child! And I turn the knob and press.

And the door doesn't move. The knob spins freely and unlatches nothing, and the door doesn't move.

Nor does the next or the next, or the one across from it. None of the doors open and the hall goes on for ever.

There is no one. The hall dims out of sight in the distance and the two brass lines stretch into the black and fade.

This is not at all what I expected. In fact, I expected nothing, nothing at all.

DYLAN MARLAIS THOMAS

Thomas was born in Swansea, Wales, October 27, 1914. As a consequence of alcoholism, he died on November 9th, 1953. He was considerably prolific during his short life, but was subject to criticisms both glowing and vicious. His body of work was known for it's emotional impact, but was derided by some as "sibylline ravings". (Masterplots, digests of world Literature, Vol. 3, Pg. 622, Curtis Books, MCMXLIX)

That Thomas was of Welch ancestry is significant in that his work was geared toward the spoken language. He is most noted for the readings of his own works. The Welch have long been known for their oratory prowess and Thomas wrote from that point of view. His works not only had extraordinary emotional impact produced through diction, but also held to a form and structure that framed his words in a manner conducive to eliciting emotional response. He wrote, in his early works, with a sense of surrealism and personal fantasy that made his work obscure, to some. It was the universality of his later works that drew his greatest acclaim. It is, here, again, attributable to his Welch ancestry, that his works are more appreciable when heard rather than read.

Limited biographical information precludes anecdotal delineation of his eccentricities; however, it is safe to say that had his problems. The safety lies in that he drank himself to death. He personified a romantic, if stereotypical image of a true Welshman in that he was silver tongued and of stout heart, that he would cry at the birth of a child, yet take off a man's head for the wrong word. His works show almost a prescience of modern days in his transition from introspective writings into works that view humankind as a whole. Note that his style shifted coincidently with the end of World War II. That he saw himself as part of the whole rather than continuing to suffer from that terminal uniqueness common to alcoholics, is evident in his later works. This change in perception does not infer that he suddenly became well. It only demonstrates mood transition.

Mood transition, in and of itself, is not indicative of disorder. Extremity and frequency, however, can be. I found no evidence to support the idea that Thomas suffered from severe depression or bipolar disorder beyond their connection with alcoholism. This brings up the question of the relationship between alcoholism and depression. It's the same old question of the chicken or the egg, which came first. We can ask whether he was born with a gene that manifest itself as depression, as being creative, or as inducing an addictive personality. There is no black and white answer. Beyond the anecdotal, our Touched With Fire text offered nothing on the matter. We can speculate, but that's all we can do.

Speculative diagnosis may include persistent cyclothymia, but should not be limited to that, based on information at hand. It is apparent that he went on into a pathology beyond cyclothymic only once and it killed him. His death at his own hand may be construed, by some, as indicative of severe depression. It can also be seen as the result of stupidity. Who is to say whether or not he chose to take his own life? Could he have been so distraught with the human condition that life held no value for him, or did he just drink so much that his body shut down? There is no clearly defined causal relationship between alcoholism and depression. In the case of Thomas, there is no documented medical record of psychiatric treatment. We can only guess at what his demons really were.

Dylan Marlais Thomas wrote from the compassionate side of his personality. Upon acceptance of his role in his society he was able to write passionately about a subject he was no longer separate from. He was able to show concern for all humankind along with himself. The psychological trauma World War II inflicted on Thomas was a boon to literature, while, at the same time, probably , in the long run, deprived the world of one of it's best poets.

THE FLOWERS OF SAN MARCOS

There is a village buried in the jungle, half a days walk from the Plaza. It is the ruins of San Marcos, It's ancient and long abandoned and the plants have pulled down most of the stone. It is said, by the old ones, that the most beautiful flowers in the world were grown in San Marcos. The old men also say that the girls who brought them to sell at the market were the most beautiful girls in the world.

"And what happened to these beautiful girls?" we ask. "Where have the people gone?"

The old ones shake their heads and say we must not speak of them.

Many of us have seen the flowers of San Marcos, how they blaze in the sunlight and dance in the gentle breeze. Many of us have lost our senses, been overwhelmed by the scents. We ask, among ourselves, "Why did they leave? Why has the jungle taken back the earth where stood the source of such delight?" The Elders, the old ones know the story.

We, the young, the strong. We who will lead tomorrow , we ask again, "What happened there in the forest? Where have the great beauties of the world gone, these flowers and these maidens?" "Why does no one bring flowers from San Marcos to sell on the Plaza?

After many years and many pleadings, they finally relented. The old ones sat us down and told us the story. They spoke in turn, one picking up where the other left off, and they spoke long into the night. With the sun still below the horizon, we shivered as the legend came to its end.

Many, many years ago, before the Spanish came, we spoke another language. In those days, we worshipped other Gods and lived in peace. San Marcos, in those days was called House of Sun and Colors. It is said that a man and his wife found a large clearing in the jungle. There was much rock with which to build a house and the grass that filled the circle was sweet, the soil rich and black. They built a home and he grazed cattle to sell at the market. She took seeds and cuttings from the edge of the tree line and grew flowers of the most spectacular variety.

She was almost magic, and she coaxed the most fragrant of blooms. From her garden came all colors and sizes, all patterns and shades. At the plaza she sold all the flowers she could grow and her name soon spread 'round the country. People from all over sought her lovely plants. Her husbands cows did not bring in as much money as did her exotic blends. He sold his herd and made the garden bigger. They planted and bred and cross-bred all the flowers they could find. They fed their garden whatever they could and replenished the earth, even with their own blood, and their flowers grew and sold and they were happy.

They had four sons along the way. These four sons married four girls from here, the four most beautiful girls in our village. The sons and their wives worked in the garden and made it bigger and bigger and more and more beautiful flowers came from the village of San Marcos.

The sons and their wives replenished the earth with their blood too and the flowers grew and sold and they were happy. As the years went by the flowers from San Marcos became larger. Their colors grew brighter and their stems, much stronger. After so many years, it is said, the flowers from San Marcos were as tall as a man. It is said that the people of San Marcos changed over the years, too. That as the years passed, they grew younger, stronger, the women, more beautiful. And there were no children born to the people of San Marcos.

The flowers grew bigger each year and the men were more healthy each year. The women, when they came to the market each Saturday, were more and more stunning each year.

It is said that the flowers grew jealous of the women's beauty. It is said that the women were jealous of their husbands time.

When no flowers came to market from San Marcos, a runner was sent to ask. The old ones tell us he found no one in the village, that the flowers had taken the houses and burst from the windows and doors.

The old ones tell us that never again did the beautiful girls of San Marcos bring flowers to sell on the plaza. And never again were the flowers on the plaza so beautiful.

THE SECOND DAY

I am naught.

I rest formless in the air, above and to the north of the crosses.

The sun touches the clouds with pink, but leaves smoke from a dozen chimneys gray in the mourning night.

Still in shade, my body, my former body sags all the more without me within.

The muscles of my arms, of his arms, have gone lax.

The tendons have stretched and snapped. Flesh has torn.

My knees can no longer hold me and they bend in frozen collapse, the spikes hold firm.

My head, his head is bowed.

Why hast thou forsaken me?

We were close. We had them believing and caring. The Romans saw the weakness in their way, they would have come round.

Yet you let them take me. You let them beat me with words and staffs. You let them defile me in your name and allowed them to blindly hate.

You let them kill me, your son?

What good was the work I did if for that work my reward was a tortured death?

I had better been an ass with no thought beyond the load I carried, or a crow only searching for food.

Was it not your blood in my veins? Were they not your words in my mouth?

Then why have you let me, let him, come to this end?

Will my death give my followers reason to stay?

Can I serve better in death than I have in life?

There was so much more I had to do, We had to do.

There was so much more I wanted to know.

Now look at me, at him.

Two years ago he was a healthy young man in the prime of his life, ...my life. Now, bruised, bloodied and emaciated, beaten down to the ground and then nailed to that tree,

degraded, defamed, cursed, spat upon like a common criminal,

is this what you left me to face? Why?

I gave those people your words.

I lived the life of forgiveness and compassion.

I kept the pleasures at bay and thought not of my joy, but of theirs, of yours.

In my death your words will lose their meaning.

Your promises will be seen as lies.

My death will make my life worth nothing.

For you, I will not even have a son to carry my name.

When the birds have picked my bones clean, and the people I've touched have withered with age and died, there will be no memory of Christ, The Son of God.

No one will carry your words.

Northwestern New Mexico, on the edge of the Colorado Plateau, is a land of paradox. A land in and of transition. Caught between the mountains of Colorado and the Rio Grande valley, it bears the highlights of the harsh desert, yet, much of it is vertical. Here, where the sand is pressed to stone and thrust up into the sky, is a gateway to soaring mountains.

Vast canyons with walls like crumbling stairs step up, layer upon layer, till they reach the horizon. Walking these canyons is like stepping into antiquity. Wind and water have carved this rock, and sun and blowing sand continue the work, today.

Perspective is everything in this country. What you see will depend on how well you look. A strange enchantment, here, has turned horrid monsters to stone. Eyeless sockets stare from skulls of sand at landslides frozen in time. Wind carved towers, in fantastic shapes stand guard over jagged dungeons.

What lives here is strong. It must be to survive the blazing sun, little rain and the incessant wind. This is the land of the Yucca and cactus, of Sage, Cedar and pinion. These are hardy and brave the elements well. They are food and shelter. Centipedes and beetles, Rattlers and tarantulas, these live here, along with the coyote and deer. From lizard to Elk, from Eagle to Ant, we all abide here by HER leave, so close, always so close to perishing in HER glare.

Food is scarce for the wild. They must travel far to find enough to eat. Even farther for water. They are lean and hungry, and move faster than sight.

There is a poetry to the high desert. It is the verse of epochs, of eons. It's been carried in the wind forever and it's meter is etched in the scalloped sky. Stanzas of rock tumble down disintegrating slopes like notes falling off the page, and deifiable monoliths balance unbelievable on points of sand like profound philosophies based on single ideas.

Like epic poetry tends, there is a repetitiveness to the sand and sage and rock. There is a sameness to the blue of the sky and the green of the pinion. There is monotony in the Sun. Yet, no more dramatic was Ulysses tied to the mast than the tortured Juniper growing through stone. And no more foolish was Icarus than the tree that splits the cliff from which it grows.

The rhythm, here, is set by the Sun. And, here, it IS carved in stone. From slight hollows worn in towering bluffs to elegantly arched bridges, the Sun calls the tune. It is SHE who calls the wind and conducts the symphony of the sands. The rain freezes white in HER angled gaze and palisades shiver and fall at the wave of HER baton. Majesty is here in towering pillars of stone, and sudden cliffs inspire awe in the mortal.

Prophecy is here, too. Through extrapolation we envision the end: The mountains will be scoured to the Earth, and the sands, rise up like the tide.

SPIRITS

There is a place in the southern Rockies where spirits dwell,

a land of sun and wind, a place where time has stopped.

here they pace and wander, and search for the lives they've lost,

through this vacant and silent land.

Their pleas go unanswered, their calls, unheard as they shuffle from pillar to post,

yet leave no track in the sand.

They cry to their families and beg of their gods, still, no word comes to their ears.

There is no pain. There is no sickness these ghosts suffer, only the silence of no reply.

It is their lot to seek truth and understanding in this windswept desert,

the truth of their insignificance, understanding of their worldly worth.

They will remain trapped here 'til they speak the truth to themselves,

and find the understanding of the end.

How many lives have they touched, and how many tears have they caused?

Was their world brighter while they lived, or is it brighter now?

It is a given, in life they took. Did they give back or did they share?

Was theirs the touch of the healer, or did they lash out to hurt?

They will wander this earth untouched and untouching for as long as it takes

and there will be no peace for these until they've accepted their end.

They have lived their lives and touched who they would and now their day is done.

There is no second chance, no recourse. What they've done, they've done and it cannot be changed now.

The peace of final death will be welcomed when there is no regret, when there is no fear.

And that peace will be eternal when they find that truth, and understand the die that has been cast.

and these lost and searching souls or spirits will finally wink........out.

OLD DOG
WHO ARE YOU AND WHAT DO YOU WANT, HERE?

The dog stands at the door, back bristled and tail slightly awag,

"Who's there?" he seems to say and yet, there's been no knock.

"Oh, go to bed, old fool, it's just the wind." and I wrap myself more tightly.

Now, at the window, he snuffs the curtain aside.

With ears up, he rests his chin on the sill and "Nuff"s at the ghost on the porch.

"Come here, old son. Sit with me by the fire. Leave it to the winds and the cloudy night to dance across the forest. Our bones are old and tired and we don't know the tune anymore."

 Quiet whine escapes as he paces across the floor, something urgent, something wrong.

At the door, a whine again, a tentative paw, and pace.

"Come, come, old boy. There's nothing there, nothing there for you.

The rabbits are fast and the others will leave you behind.

Come here, old boy, Let the fire chase the pain from your hips."

But, no. He turns to me and skips, that skip of the aged when their heart still wants to play.

He begs me in silence, with lolling tongue and flashing faded eyes, "I must go."

And, for a moment, he's a pup again.

Outside he raises his nose to the wind, searching, searching. With the stridence of the dutiful soldier, he trots his perimeter. A stop, here, a sniff there and a good scratch to let 'em know he came by.

Then, back to the deck, and the stairs get harder and harder each time.

"Good boy, good boy. Now you stay out here and guard this place. Don't let anyone slip by, ... you wake me if they show up.

Until then, lie down and rest your head. Drift to sleep and recall the days of your youth.

Remember the warmth of the sun and the bite of the chill winters wind. Relive the joy of the chase and feast anew on the spoils.

Sleep, old boy, sleep.... Dream your dreams....

The buck raised his head quickly from the grass. Standing to his full height, he looked around carefully. His large, tufted ears pivoted around behind his antlers as if they had eyes of their own, searching for the sound. It was nothing. He checked to see where his does had wandered and found them grouped together in a small stand of Pinon. The two new young ones, product of last years rut, grazed beyond the trees soaking in the last of the sun's warmth.

The cross-hairs in Michael's scope settled gently on the shoulder of the massive Mule Deer as he dropped his head back to the ground and continued his evening meal, oblivious to the two men who watched and waited.

"Boy, doesn't he look healthy?" Gary grunted assent and repositioned himself. "By the look of things, I'd say he's going to have a warm winter, too." Michael's voice practically dripped with satiric envy, "Some guys have all the luck."

It would soon be dark, but not soon enough. Michael and Gary lie prone in another stand of pine some four hundred yards south of the small herd. They had been there since before dawn and both had slept for a few hours. Now, both were stiff and sore and ready to be on the move again. But they had to wait until full dark. It wasn't deer they hunted, it was man. It was one man in particular they sought; one Benny Greenwood and he, too was equipped with a scope.

Yesterday afternoon he'd watched a young man through that same scope. He watched while the man knocked on Linda's door and waited. He watched as the door opened and Linda and this stranger talked. In the cross-hairs he saw his fiancee take the stranger by the arm and laughing, gently pull him into the house. Hours later, Benny watched as the man left Linda's house. It was hard for him to keep his breathing even as the stranger walked jauntily away, down the street.

Willing his muscles to relax and his heart to slow had been difficult. By the time he'd stilled his shaking hands, the stranger was out of sight. Benny lurched to his feet and scrambled to the top of the hill where his truck was parked. He knew where the stranger was going. He'd seen the bright red sports car in the parking lot of the Wayward Inn. Benny drove there as fast as he could. The motel sat in a wooded lot at the west end of town, surrounded by white board fencing. When Benny arrived, the lot was empty. He scanned the hillside west of the motel and found a good place from which to sight in on the stranger's door. Benny had checked. The man stayed in room seventeen.

Benny estimated the range to the door of room seventeen to be about eight hundred yards and was pleased to see the numbers so close he could almost touch them. The scope had been a good investment. He waited for almost an hour before the little red car pulled into the lot. The stranger parked in front of his room door and seemed to take forever to get out of the car. When he finally did, it was only a few quick steps to the door. Benny watched as the stranger fumbled with his key-card for a moment, then the door was open.

The crack of the rifle was painfully loud in the quiet afternoon air. The impact of the bullet tumbled the stranger headlong into his room and the door bounced back off the wall and caught at his foot. It stayed open, inviting anyone to look at the horror inside.

Benny had run, then. Run back to the hills where he'd lived most of his life. The gunshot had attracted some attention and his truck had been identified coming down off the hill. Now, the police and half the men from town were out looking for him. He was armed and dangerous, according to the cops, and was now a fugitive from justice.

Michael and Gary had known Benny all their lives. They knew he wasn't too tightly wrapped and were worried that he might do something stupid and get himself shot. Both men trusted Benny not to shoot at them under normal circumstances, but once Linda came into the picture, things changed. Benny was crazy about that girl and now that he'd already shot one man, they weren't going to take any chances. Nobody was. Gary just hoped they'd find Benny before anyone else did. He had hopes that he could talk him in to giving himself up before anyone else got shot.

It was dark, now. Gary and Michael moved through the brush with animal silence. They communicated with hand gestures as they approached Benny's lean-to and as they got to within twenty feet or so, Gary called softly. "Benny. . . Benny, It's Gary. Me and Mike are out here and we want to talk with you." Silence. "C'mon, Benny, we know you're in there. Come on out and let's talk before the cops get here."

"You boys better get on out o' here. This got nothing to do with you. This is between me and the law."

Frustrated, Michael hissed back, " Damn it Benny, there's people all over these hills lookin' for you and they aren't out here to talk. They find you and some trigger-happy fool is going to blow you away."

"I know that." The tears rung in Benny's voice. "This ain't none of your business, boys and I don't want to shoot either one of you, but if you don't get out of here, I just might."

"Oh don't be stupid Benny. You aren't going to shoot us. Listen, we can get you a good lawyer out of Atlanta and you can plead insanity. There's plenty of folks around town that'd back you up."

"I ain't crazy and you know it. I just can't take that girl screwing around on me."

"Wait a minute, Benny. You think Linda was sleeping with that guy?" Gary was incredulous. "Of course she was. What did you think they was doing, playing tiddly-winks?"

"Benny, Benny, wait a minute. That guy was Andrew Paulson. He wasn't screwing around with Linda. He likes boys. He works in that upholstery shop over in Elmira. He's recovering Linda's furniture.

"Oh, Shit. Is he dead?"

"No, he ain't dead, but he's madder'n hell." Mike threw in with a chuckle. "I guess you winged him pretty good."

Gary shushed him and called out to Benny "Andy thinks you shot him 'cause he's gay."

"Because he's what?

"Gay, you know, queer, likes boys more than girls."

"If he likes boys more than girls, what the hell was he doing laughing and cutting up with Linda and going into her place all lovey-dovey and all?

"I told you. He's recovering Linda's furniture. You know how she hates that brown couch. Well, she's getting it covered in something else and Andy is the one that's doing it."

"Christ, the way folks in town freaked out, I thought sure I'd killed that poor son of a bitch. I was just going to shoot that silly-ass rainbow patch off his shoulder. I couldn't get my hands to stop shaking."

"Well, he's isn't dead. He was screaming about attempted murder and hate crimes in the back of the ambulance. I could hear him over my scanner." "I guess he got the cops all stirred up thinking you tried to kill him. Me and Mike knew it though. We knew that if you'd wanted to put a bullet through that man's heart, you would've done it. I heard the call go out on the radio for an ambulance so I listened to the whole thing. I heard that some guy at the motel got shot in the arm and passed out and then I heard that somebody saw your truck coming off of Tanner's hill. Then this guy wakes up in the bus and throws a fit about he's going to sue everybody right down to the dog-catcher and talking about homophobic hill-billies. That got Billy in the bus all riled up and he got on the radio and told the cops there was a madman running around shooting queers and the chief heard it. Well, he came unglued..

"That's enough!", mike shouted, "Benny you come out here and bring me your gun. If somebody else sees you with it, they're going to shoot first and ask questions later. Half the damned county's out looking for you and everybody's got a gun. You give me your rifle and we'll tie your hands behind your back and lead you out of here. We do this any other way and somebody's going to shoot you before we can get you to the cops."

Benny wasn't overly bright, but he wasn't a complete fool. He'd shot a man he thought was having a fling with Linda and it turned out that he'd been wrong. Now the police and the whole damned town were out gunning for him and he didn't know what to do.

"Gary, maybe I'd do better just shooting myself and getting it over with."

"I don't want to hear that kind of crap, Benny. We can get you out of this, but you need to give me your gun first and then we'll walk out of here and give you up to the police."

Benny saw a way out. He knew it was a long walk to where the closest cars could be parked and he also knew that Fullers Run was about half way there. He might be able to make a break for it once he got there. Nobody would follow him down Fullers Run. He trusted Mike and Gary, but he didn't trust any of the rest of them. He'd known most of the men in town all his life and he knew that something as big as this would bring out all the Loonies. He could hear the dogs in the distance and could almost smell the beer.

24

"O.K., I'm coming out, don't shoot!" Benny opened the door of the shack and leaned his rifle against the porch rail. He put his hands over his head and marched stoically toward the trees where Gary and Mike were hidden.

"I knew you'd do the right thing. Go ahead and put your hands down, we're not going to shoot you." Gary stood and pointed his rifle at the ground.

Benny was scared, a lot more scared than he was willing to let on. He'd already heard one gun shot and he knew that, sure as hell, somebody'd take a pot shot at him as soon as they saw him. Mike and Gary had heard the shot, too and worried about the same thing. After some discussion about whether Benny should be tied up it was decided that doing so would be safer for him. After all, who'd shoot a man with his hands tied behind his back? Once that had been decided, there was a moment of confusion when it was discovered that there was no rope with which to tie his hands. Gary found an old roll of Duct-tape in the shack, but there was so little of it left that they were forced to tear it into strips which proved only long enough to secure his thumbs together. The tape was old and dried out and Benny was pleased that, when the time came, he'd be able to free his hands with just a bit of a tug.

The long walk back started well enough and the three friends carried on fairly bright conversation. As they got closer and closer to Fullers Run, Benny became more and more agitated. So as not to give himself away he kept his head down and said as little as he could get away with. Mike and Gary assumed that it was nerves on Benny's part that left him so morose. Both men understood. Conversation soon died and the trio walked in silence through the oppressive darkness

Fullers Run is a cleared strip of land that runs down the side of a mountain. Back in the fifties Ma Bell had run telephone lines all over these hills and one particular stretch had acquired not only a name, but a reputation throughout the county. Kenny Fuller, a sweet boy of fifteen years, had seen the clear-cut strip from the top and thought it would be fun to ride down it in a barrel. He was sweet, but he wasn't too quick. It took him half the day to roll the barrel up to the top of the hill and about thirty seconds to get to the bottom. It was only the fact that Kenny had brought his two best friends with him that saved his life. The barrel rolled easily with Kenny inside it and picked up speed surprisingly quickly. By the time it had traveled a hundred yards, the boys knew they'd made a mistake. Kenny was so disoriented that all he could do was push against the sides to keep himself from being dashed to death. In just a few seconds he'd realized the error of his ways. The strip was much steeper than he'd thought and the barrel rolled much faster than he'd expected. He was also surprised at how flat the strip wasn't. There were downed trees and boulders strewn along the whole way and soon the barrel was bouncing and spinning like a pinball. With each crash and bang the boys winced as they watched their companion fairly fly down the hill. For more than a quarter of a mile, Kenny rolled and bounced and spun from tree to rock to stump. With each bump that sent the cask sailing into the air, the boys expected to see it disintegrate, to see their friend thrown, battered and bloody, to his death. By some miracle, Kenny survived the trip. The last fifty feet had to set some kind of record. The fact that the barrel remained intact for the whole journey to that point should be some kind of record in it's self. As it was, the wooden projectile struck a stump and bounced some twenty feet into the air only to be stopped by a telephone pole that stood in the middle of the track, at the bottom of the hill. The barrel shattered like a thrown egg and Kenny was spilled on the ground much like any egg thusly destroyed. A full body cast and a wheel chair, a few missing teeth and a broken nose kept Kenny away from the mountain for six months. Soon after that his family moved away and Kenny became legend.

Benny was amused by the idea that only he and Kenny would be known for making it down Fullers Run. Nobody else had tried it. He wasn't going to go down it in a barrel, though. He was going to run. He didn't think Gary or Mike would shoot at him and he figured that with just a little light, he'd be able to see well enough to miss the obstacles on his path to freedom. With that in mind he asked Mike if he'd mind if they sat for a while and rested.

There was no objection and the three men sat in a clearing. Gary looked around himself and got his bearings. He could tell that they had stopped just to the west of Fullers Run. It didn't occur to either him or Mike that Benny might try to escape, let alone make an attempt at Fullers Run. Benny knew it and bided his time till the moment was right. Then, in the blink of an eye, he was gone.

It wasn't so dark that he couldn't be seen, but the trees and underbrush made keeping up with him almost impossible. First he ran west and then dropped behind a rock only about fifty yards away.

Mike and Gary were after him in seconds and because of their yelling and swearing, didn't hear that he'd stopped. Mike actually jumped off the rock that Benny hid behind and went crashing through the brush, still heading west. Benny's prayers were answered. With both pursuers moving away from Fullers Run, he took the chance and bolted east and back through the clearing where they'd rested. His plan worked perfectly. At the top of the Run, Benny could see the trees and rocks that had been Kenny's peril. With animal grace, he leapt from the crown and began his sideways decent. He had learned as a young child that it was not safe to run straight down a hill. Like most children, he learned this lesson the hard way. Over the years he'd become quite proud of his skill at jumping sideways to get down hill. He tried to separate his hands, but couldn't and was, therefore, left with little to help him maintain his balance. In short order he lost it and became a projectile, himself. He rolled and bounced and flew and bounced again, and again till he reached the bottom. There, in a pile of nothing but pain, he came to a halt, his thumbs securely taped together. His last conscious thought was that he was only the second person to make it down Fullers Run.

CHAP. II

Both Gary and Mike were furious at having been duped so easily, especially by someone of Benny's caliber. They met up with some of the other hunters and formed a group to chase Benny toward town. Soon full daylight was upon them and the heat was withering. Having run out of both beer and motivation, most of the hunters gave up and headed home for some sleep. For Mike and Gary, anger had replaced the fear that someone would shoot Benny. Now, either of them might shoot him. By noon both men were exhausted. No food, little sleep and the frustration caused by the failure of their mission had so discouraged them both that they gave up the hunt and went home to bed.

Being Chief of Police in his little back-woods town had always been a source of pride for Eddy Joe Ralston. He never let anyone forget that he'd been reelected to the position five times. Never mind that no one had run against him in four of the past five elections. Never mind that the only person to challenge him had been some city-slicker from Atlanta who'd made his dot-com fortune at thirty four years old and retired to the country. Chief Ralston ran a tight ship. He had three deputies and a holding cell and spent his days either sleeping at his desk or sleeping behind the wheel when he had to go out and man the speed-trap. Every now and then he'd have to send one of the deputies out to break up a fight at Smelly's Bar or chase someone's pig off the road, but, for the most part, Dayton was a quiet town. Chief Ralston liked it that way and tended to get snippy when things went amiss. Today things were amiss. He and two of his deputies had been out all night looking for Benny. Eddy Joe hadn't really expected to find him, but had thought it best to keep an eye on the self-proclaimed posse, what with the booze and all. They had met up with Gary and Mike just after sun-up and found that Benny had been both caught and lost somewhere in the woods north of town. That was the beginning of his bad day. Next, he found that Billy had taken the day off because he'd worked the ambulance last night. Granted this was the right thing to do under normal circumstances, but, things were not normal, today. That left Eddy Joe with no choice but to man the desk at the station.

The first call woke him at a few minutes after ten. It was a reporter from The Elmira Star. He told the chief that a man named Paulson had contacted him with a story about attempted murder. He asked the Chief to verify the tale. It took Ralston a minute to wake up. It took him another minute to decide how to answer . After going over his options in his mind he chose to fall back onto that old standard of not being able to comment on an on-going investigation. The reporter went on to say that Mr. Paulson claimed he was shot because he's gay.

"Because he's gay? No, I'm sorry, you've got some wrong information."

"Then, can you tell me why he was shot?"

"I can't comment on that."

"Can you tell me who shot him?"

"No, I can't answer that, either."

"How often do hate-crimes like this happen in your little town?"

Chief Ralston thought over this conversation many, many times over the ensuing years. As soon as the words fell out of his mouth, he knew he'd said the wrong thing. In his mind, the response was perfectly justified. He'd been up all night. The call had awakened him from a very deep sleep. His legs were tired and his ass was sore. He was hungry and to top it all off, the reporter was rude and pushy.

"Oh bullshit." and then punched off his phone.

That was the first of forty-three calls the Chief took that day. At five o'clock he turned the contraption off. There were thirty two red pins sticking in the Chief's county map. A tablet lay on his desk which was covered with names and locations and times. There had been calls from reporters as far away as Macon and every one of them asked about the hate-crimes. Eddy Joe looked at the map and desperately hoped that Benny was far away from his quiet little town by now. He'd had all day to get away and he knew his way around these hills as well as anyone. With any luck at all, Benny would just keep running right on out of the state.

There had been thirty-three reported sightings but only thirty-two pins stuck in the map. Hettie Larson, out on 218 had called in twice and given him the same story. She'd seen Benny sneaking around her back yard. It wasn't until Deputy Ansel called in on the radio that Eddy Joe remembered Mrs. Larson's back yard was swampland. There was no place to hide. Flat, stagnant water spread for miles from the back of Hettie's house. Nothing grew over six inches tall and the whole area was aswarm with mosquitoes. Even Benny knew better that to go out there. Deputy Ansel thought Hettie might just be lonely.

One of the things about a small town is how fast word travels. Another is the tendency small-townsfolk have for overreacting to purportedly newsworthy events. Everyone in town knew that Benny had shot somebody. Everyone in town knew that he was running from the law. To Chief Ralston, it seemed that almost everyone in the county had seen Benny. At ten thirteen, Joe Ridgly called in to say he'd seen Benny in his truck out on Highway 20, two miles east of town. No sooner had Eddy Joe hung up when the phone rang again. This time it was Mrs. Levine. She saw Benny at the Kmart on Branch street. He was pulling out of the parking lot and heading west toward the freeway. Ben Clancy saw him over at the Sunoco station on fourth street and Jed Billings saw him eating breakfast through the window of Betty's Diner, on Main. At first, the Chief thought it was great that the people around here were so helpful. After putting the pins on the map where he'd been spotted and noting the times of the sightings, he realized that either there were more than one Benny or he was able to be in more than one place at a time. At noon he stopped sending Deputy Ansel to check on the calls.

CHAP. III

Benny woke in more pain than he'd ever experienced. He lay still for a few minutes, afraid to move. He opened one eye just a little to see if anyone was around and found himself alone. His gambit had worked. Now he had to hide out somewhere, but he didn't know if he could get up, let alone walk. He struggled to open his other eye and found that to be impossible. He was lying on his side with his hands behind him and he tried to sit up. After a brief but painful struggle he succeeded but his hands were still bound. It took him a full two minutes to get free of the tape and in the process, he found all the places that hurt. There were more of them than he knew he had places. He gently put his hand to his face and felt the swelling. He also felt the sticky blood drying there. He touched his nose and sent a bolt of fresh pain across his face. His nose didn't feel like it was where it should be so he gently pushed it back over.

He woke a few minutes later with a start. It seemed that readjusting his nose had helped bring his true situation into focus. He was a wanted man. He was at the bottom of Fullers Run. He was about five miles from town and another two from his house. He'd left his truck at the campground, but that didn't matter. He couldn't drive the truck anyhow. He was hot and sweaty, he hurt all over, he was hungry and real thirsty and he had to get out of the open. If he hadn't been so scared of getting shot, he would have sat there and cried. Fear got him to his feet and he made an ungainly break for the trees. The shade helped clear his mind. It was a little cooler and the sun didn't hurt his eye, there. He'd lost his hat somewhere along Fullers Run and thought only for a few moments about retrieving it. He felt naked without it and just knew there were people out there with guns looking for him. It broke his heart to leave it behind, but, in a moment of clarity, had realized that going after it could be fatal. He rested for a few minutes, then set off limping toward town.

Andrew Paulson was released from Dayton County Hospital twenty one hours after he entered the emergency room. He was livid. He was sure he was going to die of some kind of blood poisoning or infection he'd caught from the E.R. And the ride in the ambulance had terrified him. The medics in the van had acted like teenagers with the siren and lights and squealed around corners and went flying over bumps. Then, at the hospital, they acted like he was some kind of sissy going into hysterics about his arm. Somebody'd practically blown it off and they weren't even concerned. He panicked when they released him and threatened to sue if they didn't admit him. He'd spoken to his doctor and his lawyer. The E.R. doctor had spoken to his doctor and his lawyer and so had the presiding CEO. Andrew was still miffed that they hadn't put a bigger bandage on his shoulder. At seventeen minutes after five he walked up to the counter of Sam's Pawn Shop and told Sam he wanted to buy a gun.

It took only a few seconds for Sam to size his customer up. He had Queer written all over him. From the dainty walk to the gentle lisp and the impeccable dress, Sam saw dollar signs galore.

"Well, I've got a few, here, what are you looking for?"

"Oh, I don't know, something big.

"What are you going to shoot?"

"Well, a bear or something, whatever comes after me."

"A bear, huh? Well I got a .45 over here that'll knock down a bear, but, it's a pretty big gun and there aren't too many bears around here."

"Fine, I'll take it, Just put it on my American Express."

Sam took a deep breath and let it out slowly. " You know there's a three day waiting period before you can pick it up?"

THE ORATOR

The days of the orator are returning.

They shall be men and women of all tribes of the Earth, and they will share our history with us.

They will tell tales of far away places, and some will sing and some will dance and some will speak from their hearts.

Those will take us on journeys exploring our emotions, seeking the truth, the real..

Seeking that which makes us human. They will speak with voices of iced liquor and tell us what we want to hear. They will pull our heart strings and painfully close our throats. They will touch our eyes with tears.

When the curtain closes, they will count their coins. They will pack up and move to the next town and hone their skills along the way.

In the next town they will change the billing and send the dancers out first. The singers and the music makers will follow, and the speaker will finish off.

Tonight she will wow them, she'll rock 'em in their seats.

In her fluid speech, she will tell them a tale of Love and adventure, of faithful maidens in white beset by dragons, of brave suitors.

She will keep them on the edge of their seats with blazing swordplay and suspend their breath with terrifying flights. and she will touch their hearts.

With unrequited Love and abandoned children of the street, she will make them feel.

they will know the loss of a loved one, they will shiver in the cold of alone.

The grand finale will be a laugh. They will see themselves in her and laugh as she laughs, at themselves. When the curtain closes, she will count her coins and pack up to move on.

COLORES TUYOS

I choose silver to rest against your golden skin,
That silver of platinum that glitters deep in the earth,
that the sun might reflect bright stars from a warm amber sky.
and I choose blue to drape your gentle frame,
       that blue of desert skies,
that the clouds, so rare and afraid, might see they too are welcome
here.
I choose green to bind your waist,
that green of Pinion, full in the full light of summer,
that she may share her beauty and her strength.
That she may shelter you.
I choose black to grace your slender legs,
that black of moonless, starless night,
       that the silent, depthless dark of your eyes
might sparkle the coming of stars.
I choose red to touch your lips, your nails,
that red of Sangre de Cristo,
that I may taste his warmth in your kiss,
that you may feel his gentle touch rake softly down your back.
 and I choose white to bedeck your fragile wrist,
that white of snow, of distant stars,
       that it may join the dance in your eyes, ...and leap from that
sacred blood.

THE LADY AND THE SEA

She walks the shore in daylight hours with her eyes turned to the
sea.
And at night she lies alone in her bed and shares her grief
with all those who have come before.
Only they know the crushing weight of her loss.
Only they share her fury and her rage.
In younger days she'd set her cap for him.
She wooed him as only a girl in love can, and chastely let him love
her.
And all the while the sea lay in wait, her shimmer and wave calling
him,
her distant shores taking his thoughts away.
She walks the shore in the daylight hours with her eyes turned to the
sea.
and those eyes hold the hate of every woman who's lost her man to
another.
They also hold the tears.
At night she asks herself what she could have done.
How could she, of mere flesh, compete for his love
with the timeless beauty of the sea.
How could she bedeck herself
that he would see only her, and forget the distant lands.
Her mother had warned her not to love a man who loves the sea,
as had hers, and hers, and hers.
That he will ever chafe to be in his lovers arms,
that his eyes will always turn, will always search,
and that she will always call.
Bitch, whore, home wrecker, slut,
these epithets sink into the sea with no more aplomb than a cast
stone.
And the millions of cast stones have done nothing to mar her beauty,
have done nothing to calm her allure.
She walks the shore in daylight hours with her eyes turned to the
sea.
Each sail that crests the horizon sets her heart to speed,
that it might carry her love back to her,
each ship that docks holds her eyes till all have come ashore.
and still the sea keeps him.

Whether she has dragged him to another shore
 or holds him clasped to her breast in the frigid deeps, no word has
ever come.
 His children no longer know him
 his dog still seeks his scent in the wind.
She walks the shore in the daylight hours with her eyes turned to the
sea,
and if anyone should ask,
the tears are because of the wind.

THE FALL

The fall, when it came, was horrible. It started with the detonation of a homemade bomb in the terminal at Albuquerque's Sun Port. As bombs go, it was a small one, but it was vicious. Almost two hundred people were injured and one man died at the scene. He bled to death. I guess he was standing right next to it when it went off. The bomb had been assembled in a dorm room at the University campus. It's components had been sent through the mail from campuses around the country to a young Chemistry major from Balpool. It took a week to get all the parts. When the explosive and timer came in, it was hand delivered by a 15 year old punk from the South valley. The device was amazingly simple: It was made from a glass cylinder about one foot in diameter and one foot tall. Lining the inside of that were two layers of Pyrex test tubes, each half full of some kind of liquid. These were said to be everything from nerve gas and mustard gas to bio-toxins of all stripes. It doesn't matter. In the center of the ring of tubes was a larger sleeve. This was filled with a derivative of the infamous C-4 and capped with a sophisticated timer. By the time that little wild fire was put out, fourteen thousand people had died. That was in a span of about two months. People from all over the world were infected, but most cases showed up in the American Southwest.

We retaliated. We staged strikes in Syria, Iraq and Iran. Iran fired back with the one nuke they had, but they decided to hit Israel. After that, there was a lot of sabre rattling throughout Europe and then, The North Koreans got involved. They were sure we were going to attack them through South Korea so they leveled the whole country. There were nukes and bio-weapons used there. China either got gutsy or got scared and fired on the Northwest coast from submarines while, at the same time, sweeping down through Korea to the China Sea. Israel screamed Genocide and shot up the rest of the middle east and we fired on China. There were definitely Nukes used there.

The specifics are moot from then on. The coastlines were devastated. Major population centers around the world were destroyed, airports, interstate highways, hospitals, military installations, all across America, almost everything was flattened. The same held true for the rest of the planet. There was no place on Earth where the effects of the conflagration were not felt. Clouds of poisonous vapor coalesced in low lying areas. Radiation drifted with the jet stream. Small pockets of survivors were ravaged by disease until only a few hearty souls were left. These, as is the way of humans, sought out others who had survived. Most joined some form of community feeling more secure with numbers, but, there was the threat of contagion. Diseases of old had been reborn in strength and passed through the camps like wildfire. They left, in their wake, still more bodies of which to dispose. For months after the bombs had stopped there could be seen columns of grey brown smoke curling into the sky. The stench of burned flesh was everywhere and the building clouds acquired a yellowish tint.

It began raining in August. That would have been 2008. By the end of September, we had a foot of snow in the yard, We being Laura, my wife, and our four dogs. More about them later. By then, things had pretty well burned themselves out. Not only were cities burned to rubble, but vast tracts of forestland had gone up, too. Wave after wave of smoke had rolled over us with the clouds. The wind shifted constantly and never calmed. Weather came from all directions and temperatures dropped. That first winter was cold.

It was only the beginning, though. The destruction from the bombings was almost inconceivable. There were, literally, hundreds of millions of people who had survived the bombings and the first flush of disease and many had no shelter. God knows how many froze to death or starved that first year. By spring, nothing was moving. People all over the world had radios but the mad rush to rebuild had been thoroughly crushed by the cold. Influenza held on and reinfected families time and again, Hanta virus spread from town to town. Small Pox , Dysentery , Cholera, Pneumonic and Bubonic Plague, where people gathered so did these and no one was safe. That's when strangers really started becoming suspect.

I mentioned Laura, earlier. She was my wife. She survived the first winter, but died during the second. Her system just couldn't take any more. We met on a train and I fell immediately in love. We had a story-book romance and married within a year. She was pretty and she was smart and she had the patience of a saint. We disconnected from the rest of the world and got ready for this to happen. Her patience shows in that she helped me build our house and stock it with all this stuff. She went along with my self sufficiency ideas and pulled me out of some tough quandaries about what was more important. When Laura died part of me died, too. There will always be an empty space.

HOUSE OF CARDS

Set randomly on table or carpet or tile,

With no delineating foundation, construction starts.

Each piece is painstakingly put in place and rests against another,

not one can stand on it's own.

One layer across, a ground floor, even level and stiff,

And another, smaller, built inside the walls and above,

And another, and another...

And so it goes, from the child with his play toys to nations and states.

With millions and millions of lives as the cards.

They are stacked on unstable footings and subject to the winds of the world.

And they are built in the vain grandiosity of "Mine".

"This will be my house, my city, my country,

I will raise it to the sky"......

...and I will build it from the bones of those who say no.

We know this. We've seen this all our lives.

The great tower stands for a time above the rest,

Then CRASH.

In two weeks, another will take its place,

And that will be among the mediocre.

Elsewhere another will rise and sway in the breeze and glorious light,

but only for a time.

It, too, will tumble to macabre wreckage.......

If you would build, take care that your walls are sound,

But, more, be certain your foundation can support all that rests on it.

SANCTITY OF LIFE....?

Thousands of years ago, before the survival of man was assured, Life was sacred.

When man first stood above the plains and looked for lunch with new eyes,

he looked, too, for the facing eyes of the predator.

He bred in rampant numbers, as many were lost to the elements,

And many became prey themselves. His numbers were kept in check.

In time, there were no more predators to monitor his prolificacy, none free to roam the earth. Their pelts helped him fight off the winter And his numbers started to rise.

Man spread into lands formerly forbidden with the goal of conquering and spreading his seed, to overcome the Earth with his brethren, let nothing stand in his way.

To be fruitful and multiply and displace anything that might eat him with that that he might eat. And still his numbers kept rising.

Now there are no new lands to conquer. If it is livable, he lives there. If it's not, he's visited. Winter's wind doesn't push him away and summer's sun doesn't cook him. If he can walk upon it, it is his, and there are no facing eyes. At least none that aren't his own. And still his numbers keep rising.

But, in kind, so too do the number of predators rise, and now they look into the eyes of their lunch every day, saying go on, breed, breed. Bare more that I may survive, for there is no more food and we must eat your children.

Now where is the sanctity of life? Is mans life as sacred as that of the Indian cow, or that of beef on the hoof? With what aplomb and ceremony would you extinguish a life? And what of a human life?

Would that you would take similar care with creating a new one.

THE FIRST DAY OF WINTER

December 21st, the shortest day of the year;
That day when dark chases dark with barely a breath between.
and the Sun races shyly across the horizon
embarrassed it almost seems that though she look upon us with
shining eyes,
there is little warmth.
        This is truly the beginning of the year.
Henceforth each dawn she will step higher into the sky
and the darkness will run more quickly across each night.
        The moon will dance higher among the stars
and look on us with warmer and warmer eyes.
Though we've yet to feel full winter's chill
and the snow waits building in the clouds, we know the days of
rebirth are nigh
and soon a warmer wind will play across the west.
        NOW........ Gaia will sleep.
But only for a while. In her absence Winter will race across the west.
Chilling winds will roll down the sierras freezing rain to snow and
pushing it east across the desert.

        When she awakes in the spring her days will be full.
She'll busy herself with the young to see that they grow tall and
strong
and paint the landscape with splashes of bright color: green over gray
and yellow over the sand.
Occasional rivers will run deep and boil brown as blankets of white
melt in the mountains.
 The birds will stage their annual changing of the guard
 and snakes and rodents will renew the "Dance Macabre".
        Ten days late the calendar will acknowledge a new beginning.
But only for the convenience of man.
The change has already begun.

It had always been a quiet little town, stuck off in the middle of nowhere in north central New Mexico. From there, it would take as long to get to the malls of Albuquerque as it would to get to the mountains of southern Colorado. The town lies in a valley, surrounded by farms and ranches and the open space of the high desert. It is peopled with Mexican families that have been there since the days of the Spanish land grants and a few new-comers drawn by it's idyllic vistas and the shadow of Georgia O'keefe. It's too remote to be trendy and no industry attracts young workers. The few businesses in town are barely kept afloat by the locals and there is no tourist attraction. Even the Oil industry has stayed away.

Highway 64 passes through this sleepy oasis on its way to Santa Fe. From there, you can go south to Albuquerque or north to Taos or Denver. Those who work do so on the farms or commute to Santa Fe. There are many who don't and the state welfare building is always bustling.

Paul Ames ran the only Hardware store in town. It was an Ace franchise he'd bought in 1974 and since the day he'd opened for business, he'd been on the edge of going under. Philomena, his wife, understood. Together they tried everything they could think of to bring in more money. It just wasn't there. They lived, as did most of Landsburg, from paycheck to paycheck. Their house was paid for and so were their cars and the kids had all they needed. All in all, they were happy. Six days a week Paul was at the store. Phil came in afternoons when her help was needed, but that was usually at the beginning of the month, when the checks came in. Their son, Paul Jr. went to second grade at Landsburg Elementary and Alison, their vibrant five-year-old enjoyed the safe and healthy lifestyle of rural childhood.

A low ridge of ancient sandstone provides the horizon to the west of Landsburg. On cloudy nights the orange glow of Santa Fe gently paints a portion of the sky to remind us that we are not truly alone. The distances between Landsburg and the state capitol consist not only of miles, but of time and technology as well. The numbers of people and the pace of life between the two towns differ as much as if they were of separate realities.

Philomena had started her day as she had started countless others; first, the laundry and then, the vacuuming. The power-head

41

rolled over and caught something under the couch. She swore under her breath and jumped to shut the machine off. Pulling the head from under the couch, she found one of Paul Jr.'s socks wrapped around the beater-bar. The dryer hadn't eaten this one. The vacuum had beaten it to it. Phil sat down on the floor and began to take the head apart, all the while lecturing her scatterbrained son in absentia. Just as she started to put it back together again, Alison ran in from the yard and shouted, "Mommy, smoke, mommy, smoke." Phil had lived in this country long enough to know the danger of a wind-swept range fire and had taught her children to fear them. The fear in Alison's voice brought her immediately to her feet and she rushed out the front door, dragging the protesting child with her. "Where, where, where did you see the smoke, honey?" "There, Mommy, way over there." The girl pointed south, toward the Alvarado place. Phil looked where the child pointed and saw, far to the south, a slight but blossoming fluff of gray crawling it's way up into the sky.

The human mind is an amazing thing. In the seconds before she spoke again, Philomena Ames experienced a range of emotions, from heart-stopping fear to crushing relief. The smoke was too far away to be any threat, but, was billowing up enough that she instinctively knew it was not something normal. To her eye, the stain in the sky had to be at least as far away as Albuquerque, maybe even as far as the Bosque outside Belen. She'd seen smoke from such fires before. As she watched, she told Alison that the fire was too far away to be dangerous and thanked her for telling her about it. "C'mon, lets go see if we can hear anything about it on the radio."

The radio gave them nothing but static. Phil scanned from one end of the dial to the other, on both AM and FM and heard no broadcast, anywhere. She tried the television and got the same result, nothing. Cold fingers of fear caressed her heart as she went to the phone. She had thought to call Paul at the store, but, there was no dial-tone. She told herself that now was no time to panic. Hiding her fear as best she could, she suggested that she and Alison go and see Daddy at the store, Maybe he needed some help.

The drive to the store only took a few minutes. When she got there, she found that she wasn't the first to have had a problem with her radio. Others had come in the store and several were discussing the possibilities. Most of the conversation was in Spanish so only a few words were available to her ear. With these so scattered and without context, Phil could make nothing of the conversation except an air of nervous tension. Paul had no more idea than she did as to what the problem was, but, agreed with the consensus that the smoke to the south had something to do with it.

Philomena was a tall woman. Standing next to Paul, she looked of average height, yet, she towered over most of the men in the room. The ebb and flow of the conversation washed over her as she stared out the window. Spanish was a language she had yet to master and the words flew too fast for her to catch. She looked to the West, at the ridge where the sun would set, in a few hours. She could feel the tension in the air. These men were the backbone of the community. Phil knew them all and had spoken with each of them countless times. That they spoke Spanish was no affront to her; it was their language and she was new to their town. Phil scolded herself again for not putting more effort into learning their tongue. As she watched, the ridge, almost four miles away, shifted in her sight. The movement was obvious enough that her eyes instantly jumped into focus and as she looked to see what she had seen, the skyline leapt, again. Paul heard her intake of breath and when he looked to her, her eyes were wide with shock. Before either could speak, the ground beneath their feet lurched. A dozen voices stopped as one and before the silence had hit the floor, it lurched again.

Just as the first jolt had turned the voices off, the second had snapped them back on. There were cries of, "Terremoto!!, Terremoto!!", and the store was quickly vacated. Phil made the translation quickly, though, not through her linguistic prowess, but through recognition of the men's reaction. She had seen it before when she was in California. There came a sharp grinding noise as the last of the men cleared the door. A straight, diagonal crack split the front window of the store from corner to corner and plaster and dust fell from a gash in the ceiling. Paul and Philomena hastened to join the others in the street where conversation had shifted from Terremoto to incendio y humo. They waved and gesticulated toward the spine of rock and spoke of Santa Fe. Smoke climbed into the sky in gray-black, lumpy fingers from behind the sandstone horizon. The deathly bloom grew so fast that it, too, brought conversation to a close. When it started up again, it was subdued and tinged with fear. "I must go home." and "My wife's sister lives in the city."

Everyone knew it wasn't an Earthquake. Paul turned to his wife and said, "Why don't you and Ali head out to the house? I'll close up shop and go pick up Paul Jr." Paul handed Alison to her mother, then, impulsively, he grabbed them both in a great bear-hug and nuzzled in between their heads, whispering "I love you."

There was no electricity when Phil and Paul got the kids home. They tried to make a game of it and cooked dinner on the grill. They dug tents and sleeping bags out and set up camp in the back yard. Hours after the kids had gone to sleep, Phil broached the subject that had been in seclusion for most of the day. "What are we going to do?" After a few moments thought, Paul took a deep breath and replied in a voice Phil had never heard before. "I don't know, Honey. We don't know how much damage was done or what's left out there.... I don't know." Later, an old radio turned up in the garage and Paul put some new batteries in it. He got a station out of Oklahoma that was fairly clear and began to learn just how much his life had changed. There was only News and all of it was horrifying. Paul and his wife of ten years sat huddled beside the fire and listened in heartbroken silence. There were reports from all over but, the story was the same; cities destroyed, ports and airports leveled. The hundreds of warheads that must have fallen and the millions of lives... By Philomena's watch, it was almost three thirty when they decided they'd heard enough.

The following day Paul opened the store late. There was a crowd gathered in front when he arrived and the conversation was frantic. Most of it was in Spanish and beyond Paul's ken, but, he did get a few words now and then. In the time it took to unlock the door and usher the customers in, Paul had come to understand that word had spread throughout the community: Nuclear weapons had fallen on Albuquerque and Santa Fe as well as most of the civilized world. Wind would blow the radiation over Landsburg and most folks were leaving. The customers wanted ply-wood to board up their houses before they left. It was ironic that never before had he had so many customers at once. Ironic, too, was that on this day, with more business than he could handle, Paul had decided that there would be no sales. He told the men to take what they needed and apologized for not having enough wood to go 'round. He left the store open and went home to his family.

There was no reason for the Ames family to go anywhere. Neither Paul nor Philomena had any family they were close to and there was no safer place to be, so, they decided to stay. Less than twenty-four hours after they saw the smoke on the western horizon,

Landsburg was empty. Paul drove the streets to see who was left and found only those who were still packing up. He wondered how he was going to explain to the kids why everyone had left town and why they were staying. Would they understand that Landsburg was as good a place to die as anywhere?

Three weeks had passed. Paul and Phil had been busy trying to turn their house into a defensible fortress. The radiation sickness had yet to materialize and the fear of it lessened with each passing day. The kids were surprisingly accepting of their new life and pitched in to help where they could. It was almost as if they knew that their help was necessary and that it was time to forgo the irresponsibility of childhood.

Over on the other side of town, there was a group of people living in a couple of trailors. They were sort of a bunch of wanna be bikers and vandalized a lot of the town. There was no one to stop them. Paul made it very clear that he was armed by shooting targets around the house. He also started teaching the kids to shoot. The folks across town drove by now and then, but they just waved and kept going.

Paul had always been confident. He was intelligent, healthy and attractive. He and Philomena had been lovers in college and had married when she graduated. They had waited to have children until Paul got the store off the ground and then waited again to have another. As far as he was concerned, his life had been right on schedule. That had all changed on a sunny afternoon in August, however. Now he was nervous and didn't sleep worth a damn. He had never been on unstable ground in his life. It had never occurred to him how much he depended on things he didn't understand. He tried to exude the sense of self he should have felt. Inside he knew it was a sham. Thank God Philomena understood.

She had tried to explain it to the kids. Little Paul had found a dead bird in the yard and brought it to Phil, one afternoon some months back. She had tried then to explain death to him and he seemed to accept it. She now reminded him of that event and told him that many, many people around the world were dead. When he had asked why, the lump in her throat had nearly choked her. "Because they didn't think." Alison complained that she didn't understand and with tears rolling down her cheeks, Phil had pulled the child to her and kissed her cheek. "You will, my Love, you will." The children somehow knew, and left to attend to their own thoughts.

In high-school, Paul had played basketball. The team had never amounted to much and he had learned early what it was to play catch-up ball. Now his whole life was catch-up ball and there was no coach. It seemed there was always something he needed to do and he was never sure if it was the right thing. They had to have food and heat. Thank God they had a well, but, how long would it last? He took a generator from the store and wired it in to the house. There was gas at the two stations in town but the electricity was off. He could siphon gas when he needed it. Phil was learning to cook on the wood stove and there was packaged food from Albertson's stored in the basement. There were moments when Paul thought everything was under control. They were few and always superseded by his fear of the unknown

Philomena, much to her own surprise, was gaining a sense of confidence she'd never known before. Granted she'd been struck by the same tragedy as the rest of the world, but she knew, somehow, they'd be all right. Even in the short time they'd been alone she'd discovered that she really didn't miss all the people she'd thought she would. There was no time to dwell on it. They were gone and there was nothing she could do about it. There was too much work to do. Sometimes at night, before exhaustion took her, she'd think of those she'd lost and tears would flood her eyes. Those nights she'd turn to Paul and hold him tight, her face buried in his neck.

Half a century.
How insignificant is fifty years in light of the Earth's four and a half billion?
How much impact can one man have amid six and a half billion?
Who's voice is heard above the maelstrom, and who's name is recalled down the years?

Confucius, Plato, Christ, Buddha, These names have lived well beyond the men who made them famous, and been passed from generation to generation.

There are others, too. The recollection of whom brings cold to the heart and dredges up old feelings of fear: Hitler, Nero, De Sade.

Each is remembered for their gifts and the spirit in which they were given.
And though we have banished them to their proper heaven or hell, their names still stir, today.

Of course we all want to be remembered after we have passed and most of us will, by our friends and family.
 Some of us will leave progeny behind and our genes and our name will live beyond .... We will be forgotten.

Those who are recalled are so because of what they've given, or what they've taken away.
It will be our contribution that colors our name, tomorrow.

The Asp has long been known for it's deadly venom. The Orchid for it's fragile beauty.
Their names arouse silent feelings, associations of fear, of love.
The warm, luxurious scent of the gentle blossom or the evil hiss as forked tongue tastes you in the air, these we all know whether we know them or not. We've been told, down through the years, by our parents, and theirs, and theirs: The flower will give you pleasure, the viper will take your life.
It is by what they give and take that they are remembered. And so, too will we be.

When fifty more years have passed, who will remember my name? and when two hundred or five hundred, or two thousand years have flown, will my name cross anyone's lips? If so, in what context?

Will I be known as one who gave, or will I be thought a thief?
 Will my name bring light or darkness to a room?
 Of course we all want to be remembered after we've passed,
but, how so, how so?

VOTE

O.K. The party's over. American voters have spoken. President George W. Bush has been reelected and the republican party holds sway in both the House and Senate. Now is when we see what the true colors of our elected officials are. We are involved in a war in the Middle East which is the direct result of American greed and selfishness. If there had been adequate research and development in alternative energy we would have no reason to be dependant on the oil found in that part of the world. Consequently, we would not be losing American lives in the Iraq war. President Bush, in particular, and the republican party, in general profit from every increase in fuel prices we see here in America. Why do we allow it? Let us not even say anything about Halliburton and the profit the Vice President makes from their activities in Iraq. It seems to me that President Bush told the American people that the war would be paid for with oil from Iraq. Why are we spending Billions of dollars to continue it? Wasn't Vietnam enough of a lesson?

Abortion is another topic the republican party is using to distract the public from discussing the alternative energy questions. There are people in this country who would have the right of women to control their bodies taken away from them. The right-wing, conservative, religious and political leaders want to determine what is right for every American Woman. It doesn't matter that millions of unwanted babies are born into poverty. It doesn't matter that overpopulation is the root of all the worlds social problems. Just so long as those few men can flaunt their power over the masses.

Have Americans stopped thinking clearly? Do they think that global warming is a joke? Do they think taking away a woman's right to decide is a step in the right direction? Our elected officials are turning a blind eye to the most dangerous threats to the world's population. How can we justify continuing to put these people in office? As a voter, I have the right to complain. I voted my conscience. I listened to the campaign speeches and the debates and voted for the people I thought would do us the most good. To the people who didn't vote, I say you should leave our country. You obviously have no concern for it.

Gay marriage is another topic used to distract Americans from the crucial issues. America is a free country. We can marry anyone we want. If you are concerned that someone wants to marry someone else of the same sex, you have too much time on your hands. That is none of your business. Whether you like it or not, it's NONE of your business. Get your nose out of it. The facts that gay marriages tend to be as stable as heterosexual marriages are and that gay marriages do NOT produce offspring is all the justification necessary. As far as insurance goes, objection to insuring partners in gay marriages is simply another example of insurers trying to limit their coverage and increase their bottom line. There is no other reason they should object. But then, how much money did these companies give to get Bush reelected? If you really want to see who is running this country, look at campaign contributions.

These are only a few of the issues our President faces. Watch how he deals with these and take note of how much your life improves over the next four years. Look also at the pollution of our air and water. Watch your constitutional rights be taken away, one by one. Watch the fossil fuel industry persist in delaying the development of alternative energy utilization. Watch the pharmaceutical companies and the insurance companies rob Americans blind. And, most closely of all, watch who lets these things happen to us. Maybe in 2008 we will elect leaders who do care about our country. Maybe everybody that is eligible to vote will take the responsibilities that come with the rights and vote.